*To the ones that will
never be forgotten.*
H.R.

*To my grandparents
and my father.*
D.L.

**LES TIGRES
GAUCHERS**

Les Tigres Gauchers would like to thank all their valued readers.

First American edition published in 2012 by Gecko Press USA, an imprint of Gecko Press Ltd.

A catalog record for this book is available from the US Library of Congress.

Distributed in the United States and Canada by
Lerner Publishing Group, Inc.
241 First Avenue North
Minneapolis, MN 55401 USA
www.lernerbooks.com

This edition first published in 2012 by Gecko Press
PO Box 9335, Marion Square, Wellington 6141, New Zealand
info@geckopress.com

English language edition © Gecko Press Ltd 2012

Original title: Petites et grandes histoires des animaux disparus
© Actes Sud, France, 2010

Translated by Jen Craddock
Edited by Penelope Todd
Typesetting by Luke Kelly, New Zealand
Printed by Proost, Belgium

ISBN hardback: 978-1-877579-06-6

For more curiously good books, visit www.geckopress.com

HÉLÈNE RAJCAK
AND DAMIEN LAVERDUNT

SMALL AND TALL TALES OF EXTINCT ANIMALS

Scientific advisers: Cécile Colin and Luc Vives,
National Museum of Natural History, France

GECKO PRESS

CONTENTS

P.9   PREFACE

P.10   WORLD MAP

THE AMERICAS   P.12

P.14   WHO'S AFRAID OF THE MAPINGUARI?

THE GIANT GROUND SLOTH
MEGATHERIUM AMERICANUM

P.16   HOW DO YOU RECYCLE A GLYPTODON'S
BONY SHELL?

THE GLYPTODON
GLYPTODON CLAVIPES

P.18   WHO SHRANK THE GIANT BEAVERS?

THE GIANT BEAVER
CASTOROIDES OHIOENSIS

P.20   HOW DID WILLIAM CODY BECOME
BUFFALO BILL?

THE PENNSYLVANIA BISON
BISON BISON PENNSYLVANICUS

P.22   WHAT WAS MR. AUDUBON'S MOST
AMBITIOUS PROJECT?

THE GREAT AUK
ALCA IMPENNIS

P.24   WHO DID CHARLES DARWIN MEET IN
THE FALKLAND ISLANDS?

THE FALKLAND ISLANDS FOX
DUSICYON AUSTRALIS

P.26   WHO WERE THE EXTINCT BIRDS
OF HAWAII?

THE MAMO
DREPANIS PACIFICA

P.28   WHERE DID ALL THE PASSENGER
PIGEONS GO?

THE PASSENGER PIGEON
ECTOPISTES MIGRATORIUS

P.30   WHO WERE LADY JANE AND INCAS?

THE CAROLINA PARAKEET
CONUROPSIS CAROLINENSIS

P.32   WHO WAS NICKNAMED
"LONESOME GEORGE"?

THE LONESOME TORTOISE OF PINTA ISLAND
GEOCHELONE NIGRA ABINGDONI

AFRICA   P.34

P.36   IS THE TERRIBLE KILOPILOPITSOFY STILL
HAUNTING MADAGASCAR'S FORESTS?

THE MALAGASY DWARF HIPPOPOTAMUS
HIPPOPOTAMUS LEMERLEI

P.38   WAS THE GIANT ROC A GOOD WAY
TO TRAVEL?

THE ELEPHANT BIRD
AEPYORNIS MAXIMUS

P.40   HOW DID POOR OLD ITOVO BECOME
A GIANT LEMUR?

THE TRATRATRATRA
PALAEOPROPITHECUS

P.32   WHO SAVED THE TAMBALACOQUE TREE?

THE DODO
RAPHUS CUCULLATUS

P.44 # EURASIA

P.46 WHO WON THE INTERNATIONAL ANTLER CONTEST?
THE IRISH ELK
MEGALOCEROS GIGANTEUS

P.48 WHAT IS SIBERIA'S LARGEST TREASURE?
THE WOOLLY MAMMOTH
MAMMUTHUS PRIMIGENIUS

P.50 DID HERCULES SKIN THE LAST EUROPEAN LION?
THE EUROPEAN LION
PANTHERA LEO EUROPAEA

P.52 WHAT'S THE LINK BETWEEN A CYCLOPS AND A DWARF ELEPHANT?
THE SICILIAN DWARF ELEPHANT
ELEPHAS FALCONERI

P.54 WHO WERE THE INVINCIBLE AUROCHS?
THE AUROCHS
BOS PRIMIGENIUS

P.56 WHY SHOULD THE SEA COW HAVE STAYED OUT OF SIGHT?
STELLER'S SEA COW
HYDRODAMALIS GIGAS

P.58 ARE TIGERS DOOMED TO DISAPPEAR?
THE BALI TIGER
PANTHERA TIGRIS BALICA

P.60 WHEN DID THE CHINESE RIVER DOLPHIN OFFICIALLY BECOME EXTINCT?
THE CHINESE RIVER DOLPHIN
LIPOTES VEXILLIFER

P.62 # OCEANIA

P.64 WHAT WERE AUSTRALIA'S GIANT ANIMALS?
THE LONG-BEAKED ECHIDNA
ZAGLOSSUS HACKETTI

P.66 HOW DID THE WARRIOR RURU CONQUER THE LEGENDARY POUĀKAI?
HAAST'S EAGLE
HARPAGORNIS MOOREI

P.68 WHO WERE THE "MOA HUNTERS?"
THE GIANT MOA
DINORNIS GIGANTEUS

P.70 WHAT WAS THE THYLACINE REALLY LIKE?
THE THYLACINE
THYLACINUS CYNOCEPHALUS

P.72 WHOSE BAD IDEA WAS IT TO BRING A PET TO AUSTRALIA?
THE PIG-FOOTED BANDICOOT
CHAEROPUS ECAUDATUS

P.74 GLOSSARY

P.76 A FRIEZE OF VANISHING ANIMALS

THE LOST CALL OF THE TRATRATRATRA

Long before setting foot on the Moon, humans evolved on planet Earth—one continent, one ocean, one island at a time. Humans were enthralled by the world around them. To feed their fascination, they collected pictures and mementos of bones, feathers, herbariums, casts, and fossils.

Today, as a result, we have a wealth of specimens, drawings, and stories about Earth's animals. But natural history museums—that once so proudly displayed the first examples of newly discovered species—now face the unenviable task of exhibiting their remains: the last skeleton, the last skin, the last paw print, the last photograph.

The history of science is one of long, slow progress: voyages across uncharted oceans, expeditions deep into shadowy forests and far-flung lands. On each journey, the explorers were astonished by extraordinary new creatures, colors, scents, and forms. And for centuries, they followed the impulse to possess, control, and tame these newly conquered territories and the animals in them.

Nature has grown quieter than it was. The tratratratra of Madagascar has been silenced for good; this giant lemur is now heard only in folk tales and legends. Other animals whose names fire our imaginations—like the dodo, the kilopilopitsofy, the moa, and the pouākai—have suffered a similar fate.

Few books dare to touch on humanity's role in wildlife extinction. Of course, humans haven't always been solely to blame. But our impact on the environment in any given era (ancient or modern) has only intensified damage to environments already made marginal by climatic and tectonic shifts. Hunting, population growth, deforestation, and industrialization are all speeding up the rate at which plants and animals are disappearing.

We hope this beautiful book will be a record and reminder of what has been lost. Each page is an invitation to come with us on a voyage back in time.

Cécile Colin and Luc Vives
National Museum of Natural History, France

HAWAII

THE AMERICAS

PACIFIC
OCEAN

ATLANTIC
OCEAN

IRELAND

NEWFOUNDLAND

GALAPAGOS
ISLANDS

FALKLAND ISLANDS

ANTARCTIC

ARCTIC
OCEAN

BERING
SEA

EURASIA

PACIFIC
OCEAN

SICILY

AFRICA

INDIAN
OCEAN

BALI

AUSTRALIA

MAURITIUS

MADAGASCAR

OCEANIA

TASMANIA

NEW ZEALAND

OCEAN

The AMERICAS

The Americas stretch from northern Canada and Greenland to the southernmost tip of South America. North and South America are separated by the Panama Canal.

The American continent is separated from Europe by the Bering Strait. Humans first arrived here 10,000 years ago. They found the land inhabited by enormous animals like the giant beaver and the *Glyptodon*, a huge mammal encased in protective armor.

In the 1500s, European explorers crossing the Atlantic Ocean in search of a route to India came upon this land, which they named "The New World." They gradually settled here and spread out toward the west. Several animals, including the bison and the passenger pigeon, would ultimately die out as a result—direct or otherwise—of this colonization.

WHO'S AFRAID OF THE MAPINGUARI?

THE MAPINGUARI (OR ISNASHI) IS A MONSTER THAT LIVED IN THE AMAZON RAINFOREST OF BRAZIL AND BOLIVIA. ACCORDING TO LOCAL LEGEND, IT WAS A HUGE, TERRIFYING CREATURE: VERY TALL, WITH LONG ARMS, SHARP CLAWS, AND A COAT OF REDDISH HAIR OVER THICK SKIN WHICH MADE IT VERY HARD TO KILL.

IN SOME FOLKTALES, THE MAPINGUARI HAS TWO EYES; IN OTHERS ONLY ONE, LIKE A CYCLOPS. SOME TALES MAKE IT EVEN MORE NIGHTMARISH, WITH A FANGED MOUTH IN THE CENTER OF ITS BELLY. MOST AGREE IT GAVE OFF A PUTRID STENCH THAT COULD MAKE PEOPLE FAINT. THE MAPINGUARI WAS A VERY SLOW MOVER, BUT NO LESS FEROCIOUS FOR THAT.

INTRIGUED BY THESE TALES, AND BY REPORTS OF SIGHTINGS OF THIS BEAST, SEVERAL MODERN ADVENTURERS HAVE SET OFF TO EXPLORE THE FOREST IN THE HOPES OF PROVING THE MAPINGUARI EXISTS. SOME BELIEVE THE CREATURE IS IN FACT A GIANT SLOTH, WHICH WAS THOUGHT TO BE EXTINCT BUT HAS MANAGED TO SURVIVE, HIDDEN IN THE DENSE RAINFOREST.

THE GIANT GROUND SLOTH

MEGATHERIUM AMERICANUM

SIZE: 13 feet tall
WEIGHT: over 3 tons
FOUND IN: South America
DATE OF EXTINCTION:
10,000 years ago

The vast forests of the Amazon were home to several species of giant sloth: **Eremotherium**, **Mylodon**, and the huge **Megatherium**. They were ground-dwelling herbivores, in contrast to sloths now, which live in trees. Sightings of giant ground sloths are still reported today, but studies have shown that they disappeared about 10,000 years ago. If they ever lived alongside humans, it was in the distant past...

A bulky giant
The *Megatherium* was the largest of the giant ground sloths. It was 13 feet tall when it stood on its hind legs. It must have been a terrifying sight!

A hefty herbivore
The *Megatherium* lumbered through grassy plains and forests. To reach foliage high up, it balanced with its thick tail and pulled leaves toward its mouth.

A mighty plodder
The *Megatherium's* size wasn't its only weapon—it also had long claws. But this vegetarian giant wasn't aggressive and was far too clumsy to chase other animals.

HOW DO YOU RECYCLE A GLYPTODON'S BONY SHELL?

HOLA, I'M PROFESSOR FLORENTINO AMEGHINO. I'M A FAMOUS ARGENTINIAN PALEONTOLOGIST FROM THE 1800S.

A TIRELESS EXPLORER, I'VE SPENT YEARS SCOURING MY COUNTRY'S VALLEYS AND PLAINS FOR ANCIENT FOSSILS.

IN TIME I'LL DISCOVER PREHISTORIC ANIMALS THAT ARE NEW TO SCIENCE. MY FINDINGS WILL EXCITE RESEARCHERS AROUND THE WORLD AND ADD TO OUR KNOWLEDGE OF THE PAST.

ONE OF MY MOST AMAZING FEATS WILL BE REASSEMBLING THE COMPLETE SKELETON OF A STRANGE ANIMAL THAT LIVED IN SOUTH AMERICA 10,000 YEARS AGO, THE GLYPTODON.

MY PAINSTAKING STUDY OF THIS MAMMAL'S REMAINS WILL TEACH ME A LOT ABOUT HOW AND WHERE IT LIVED, AND WHAT IT ATE.

THE DISCOVERY OF HUMAN REMAINS AMONG THE GLYPTODON FOSSILS WILL CONFIRM THAT THE FIRST HUMANS LIVED SIDE BY SIDE WITH THIS ANIMAL.

IT IS EVEN POSSIBLE THAT HUMANS USED THE GLYPTODONS' GIANT SHELLS AS SHELTER, OR AS TOMBS.

THE GLYPTODON

GLYPTODON CLAVIPES

Over the course of several ice ages about 10,000 years ago, some large mammals died out. They included the **American mammoth**, the **smilodon** (or saber-toothed tiger), and the *Glyptodon*. The *Glyptodon* was a giant armadillo that lived in the South American savannahs and had a spectacular shell that protected it from predators. It disappeared in part because of the arrival of a new predator—humans.

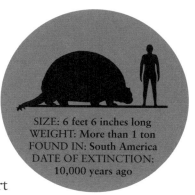

SIZE: 6 feet 6 inches long
WEIGHT: More than 1 ton
FOUND IN: South America
DATE OF EXTINCTION:
10,000 years ago

A mammal with a shell
The *Glyptodon* might look like a giant tortoise but it was, in fact, a mammal. Partially hairy, it was protected by a super-strong shell made of hundreds of small bony plates.

A formidable war machine
Along with its indestructible shell, the *Glyptodon* had a club-like tail encased in bony rings and covered in spikes.

A gap-toothed glutton
Glyptodons are from the family of animals known as "edentates," along with anteaters, sloths, and armadillos. Armadillos have very few teeth. The Glyptodon had a few teeth right at the front of its mouth, which it used to grind up leaves and tough plants.

WHO SHRANK THE GIANT BEAVERS?

LONG AGO, A NATIVE AMERICAN TRIBE KNOWN AS THE MI'KMAQ MADE SUMMER FISHING TRIPS TO THE RIVER. ONE DAY, THEY FOUND THAT GIANT BEAVERS HAD BUILT A HUGE DAM WHICH STOPPED THE FLOW OF FISH. THE MI'KMAQ FEARED THEY WOULD DIE OF HUNGER AND DECIDED TO RETALIATE. BUT THE GIANT BEAVERS WERE TOO STRONG, USING THEIR TAILS TO CATAPULT THE MEN OUT OF THEIR CANOES.

THE MI'KMAQ CALLED FOR THEIR HERO KOLUSKAP TO COME AND SAVE THEM. KOLUSKAP SMASHED THE DAM TO SMITHEREENS WITH HIS CLUB. THEN HE GRABBED THE HEAD BEAVER BY THE TAIL, SWUNG HIM AROUND, AND FLUNG HIM FAR AWAY. WHERE THE BEAVER LANDED, HE TURNED INTO A MOUNTAIN. TODAY, THIS MASSIVE ROCK IS CALLED MOUNT SUGARLOAF, IN MASSACHUSETTS.

NEXT, KOLUSKAP WENT AFTER THE OTHER BEAVERS. THEY WERE SO SCARED THAT THEY FROZE ON THE SPOT. KOLUSKAP TOUCHED THEIR HEADS AND MADE THEM SHRINK. HE TOLD THE MEN THAT THE BEAVERS WEREN'T BIG ENOUGH TO BUILD HUGE DAMS ANYMORE AND WOULD NEVER DISRUPT THEIR FISHING AGAIN.

THE GIANT BEAVER

CASTOROIDES OHIOENSIS

Mi'kmaq folktales tell of titanic battles between the legendary hero Koluskap and **giant beavers**, which suggests that the beavers lived at the same time as humans. The giant beaver is thought to have died of cold and hunger 10,000 years ago, during an extreme ice age, along with mammoths, rhinoceros, and some ancient species of horse. Today, scientists also think that hunting by humans played a major role in the giant beaver's demise.

SIZE: 6 feet 6 inches long
WEIGHT: up to 220 pounds
FOUND IN: North America
DATE OF EXTINCTION:
10,000 years ago

The ancestor of the modern beaver?
The giant beaver might look similar to today's beavers, but the two are not close relations. The modern beaver is not descended from the giant one.

A tireless gnawer
Giant beavers had long incisors (front teeth) which they used to gnaw on the tree bark they liked to eat.

A rat's tail
The giant beaver had a rounded tail like a rat, not a large, flat one like the modern beaver.

How did William Cody become Buffalo Bill?

WHEN WILLIAM FREDERICK CODY WAS JUST 20, HE WAS HIRED TO SUPPLY MEAT FOR AN AMERICAN RAILROAD COMPANY. HE WENT ON BISON HUNTING SPREES TO FEED THE GANGS OF MEN BUILDING AND LAYING THE RAILROAD.

THOUSANDS OF BISON (ALSO KNOWN AS BUFFALO) WERE KILLED BY THIS FAMOUS COWBOY. IT'S SAID THAT HE EARNED HIS NICKNAME, BUFFALO BILL, AFTER HE SET A RECORD FOR THE NUMBER OF BISON KILLED IN A SINGLE DAY.

MUCH LATER, WILLIAM CODY DECIDED TO KEEP THE NAME BUFFALO BILL, UNDER WHICH HE STAGED SHOWS THAT RECREATED THE ATMOSPHERE OF THE WILD WEST: BATTLES WITH NATIVE AMERICANS, STAGECOACH ROBBERIES, AND BUFFALO HUNTS. THE SHOWS TOURED THE WORLD AND WERE A SMASH HIT: THE LEGEND OF THE "WILD WEST COWBOY" WAS BORN.

THE PENNSYLVANIA BISON

BISON BISON PENNSYLVANICUS

SIZE: 5 to 6 feet 6 inches tall
WEIGHT: 1 ton
FOUND IN: North America
DATE OF EXTINCTION: 1825

It would be an exaggeration to say that Buffalo Bill's hunting alone caused certain subspecies of bison to die out, but he did play a large part in the massacre of the bison. Bison were hunted for their meat and hide, but also for more political reasons: American settlers were trying to starve the Native Americans in order to take control of their land. Before the first settlers arrived, there were plenty of **American bison**—in the 1700s there were between 50 and 70 million. In the era of the cowboys and the conquest of the Wild West, they almost became extinct.

A bearded bison
The Pennsylvania bison (or Eastern bison) had a dark coat, a grayish face, and a distinctive beard.

Species of bison
There were four subspecies of American bison: the wood bison, the plains bison, the Oregon bison, and the Pennsylvania bison. By the end of the 1800s these last two had died out.

WHAT WAS MR. AUDUBON'S MOST AMBITIOUS PROJECT?

WHEN THE FRENCH-AMERICAN PAINTER JOHN JAMES AUDUBON DISCOVERED THE ANIMALS OF THE NEW WORLD IN THE MID 1800S, HE WAS CAPTIVATED BY ALL THE PREVIOUSLY UNKNOWN BIRDS.

HE DECIDED TO DRAW THEM ALL, AND SET OFF ON A 30-YEAR JOURNEY THROUGH AMERICA. HE COMPLETED NEARLY 400 ILLUSTRATIONS, WHICH WERE PUBLISHED IN A NOW-FAMOUS BOOK.

THESE DRAWINGS ARE ALL THE MORE PRECIOUS BECAUSE THEY DEPICT BIRDS THAT ARE NOW EXTINCT, SUCH AS THE PASSENGER PIGEON AND THE CAROLINA PARAKEET.

IN THE NICK OF TIME, AUDUBON DREW THE LABRADOR DUCK, AS IT DISAPPEARED BARELY 50 YEARS LATER. THIS SEA DUCK WAS DRIVEN TO EXTINCTION BY FISHERMEN AND SAILORS.

AUDUBON'S IMAGES OF THE GREAT AUK ARE VERY FAMOUS. HE TRIED BUT FAILED TO DRAW THIS BIRD IN THE WILD AND HAD TO MAKE DO WITH DRAWING STUFFED ONES INSTEAD.

HE DREW TWO BIRDS THOUGHT TO HAVE DISAPPEARED LONG AGO: THE IMPERIAL WOODPECKER AND THE IVORY-BILLED WOODPECKER. RECENT SIGHTINGS OF THESE BIRDS HAVE BEEN REPORTED, BUT THERE IS NO PROOF.

THE GREAT AUK
ALCA IMPENNIS

The **great auk** lived on rocky islands scattered across the Atlantic Ocean between America and Europe. Its extinction was caused by coastal dwellers, especially by fishermen who hunted it for its meat, oil, and feathers. The great auk couldn't fly to escape its predators. From the 1500s onward, great auks were killed in the millions. Although they retreated to small, more distant islands, they were ruthlessly hunted down and finally died out in the mid 1800s.

SIZE: 2 feet 6 inches tall
WEIGHT: 11 pounds
FOUND IN: The North Atlantic
DATE OF EXTINCTION: 1844

In black and white
The great auk had a black back and neck and a white belly, with a striking patch of white between each eye and at the base of its curved beak.

Another auk
The great auk should not be confused with the razor-billed auk, which is still alive. These two birds are not only different sizes, but the razor-billed auk can fly, unlike its larger relative.

A tireless swimmer
Sturdy and resilient, the great auk was a very good swimmer. It could easily spend ten months out at sea. However, it came ashore in spring to build a nest, incubate its precious egg (it laid just one a year), and look after its chick.

WHO DID CHARLES DARWIN MEET IN THE FALKLAND ISLANDS?

THE FALKLAND ISLANDS FOX

DUSICYON AUSTRALIS

The **Falkland Islands fox** or wolf, also known as the warrah, was first seen at the end of the 1600s. It was very difficult to classify, because it looked like both a wolf and a fox. In 1833, Charles Darwin gave it the classification *Canis antarcticus*, or "**Antarctic wolf.**" In 1880, the zoologist Thomas Huxley first believed it was related to the coyote. Then he decided it was more like a fox. In 1914, the animal was formally named *Dusicyon*, in the same family as the *culpeo*, a variety of fox from South America.

SIZE: 2 feet 7 inches long
WEIGHT: 165 to 220 pounds
FOUND IN: Falkland Islands
DATE OF EXTINCTION: 1876

Remembering the warrah
People in the Falkland Islands haven't forgotten this animal. The Warrah River bears its name, and there is a picture of it on the local 50-pence coin.

Funny diet for a canine
Only two types of mammals have been found on the Falkland Islands: this fox, and a mouse. It's thought that the fox must have eaten birds, grubs and insects—strange food for a fox!

WHO WERE THE EXTINCT BIRDS OF HAWAII?

SOME SCIENTISTS BELIEVE THAT IN THE PAST 200 YEARS, MORE BIRDS HAVE DISAPPEARED FROM HAWAII THAN FROM ANYWHERE ELSE ON EARTH.

FOR EXAMPLE, ALL FOUR SPECIES IN THE GENUS *MOHO* VANISHED. HAWAIIANS CALLED THESE BIRDS 'O'OS BECAUSE OF THEIR CRY.

ALTHOUGH IT WAS LONG MISTAKEN FOR THE MOHO, THE MAMO WAS AN ENTIRELY DIFFERENT BIRD. THE MAMO WAS SHY AND DRANK NECTAR, LIKE A BEE.

THE KIOEA WAS A LARGE BIRD WHICH ALSO DRANK NECTAR FROM HAWAII'S ABUNDANT FLOWERS.

THE 'O'U (*PSITTIROSTRA PSITTACEA*) WAS VERY PLUMP. IT LOVED EATING—AND IT SPENT ITS DAYS DOING JUST THAT.

THE LAYSAN RAIL, DESPITE ITS SMALL SIZE, WAS AN AGGRESSIVE BIRD THAT WOULD FIGHT OTHER, LARGER SPECIES. ITS CALL WAS STARTLINGLY LOUD.

THE MAMO

DREPANIS PACIFICA

SIZE: 6 3/4 inches long
WEIGHT: 1 ounce
FOUND IN: Hawaii
DATE OF EXTINCTION:
1900

The **mamo** was one of many nectar-drinking birds that once lived on a single island in Hawaii. It was highly prized by the indigenous people, who caught and plucked it for its bright yellow feathers, used to decorate ceremonial clothing. A single cloak could use the feathers of tens of thousands of birds. The new European and American settlers also hunted and trapped the mamo, and sold them to collectors for their feathers and their beautiful call. The bird became increasingly rare and disappeared in about 1900. Its cousin, the black mamo, suffered the same fate a few years later.

A nectar drinker
Like the hummingbird, the mamo fed on nectar. It was crazy about the pollen from the Hawaiian lobelia. Its long, curved beak allowed it to gather nectar from closed flowers.

A shy bird
The mamo lived high in the Hawaiian forest canopy and rarely showed itself.

27

WHERE DID ALL THE PASSENGER PIGEONS GO?

THE PASSENGER PIGEON
ECTOPISTES MIGRATORIUS

SIZE: 1 foot 4 inches long
WEIGHT: 10 ounces
FOUND IN: North America
DATE OF EXTINCTION:
1914

A few hundred years ago, **passenger pigeons** (which shouldn't be confused with carrier pigeons) existed in huge numbers. Their extinction in the space of a century is one of the fastest and most dramatic in history. The main reason, of course, was hunting. But at the end of the 1800s, the passenger pigeon was also the victim of a deadly virus. By that point there were already too few birds left to ensure the survival of the species. Scientists call this the "extinction threshold"—when there are too few animals to reproduce, a species is doomed to disappear.

A flying ace
The pigeon was the perfect shape for aerobatics and high-speed flying. It had an excellent sense of direction which meant it seldom got lost on long migrations.

Traveling gluttons
The passenger pigeons' migration wasn't seasonal like other birds'. It was all about food. Once the pigeons had gobbled up every last morsel in one place, they left in search of a new feeding ground.

Pie in the sky
The French name for the passenger pigeon was "tourte voyageuse." A famous Canadian pigeon meat pie came to be called a "tourte" in the birds' honor. Today, the word "tourte" is a general term for "meat pie" in French.

WHO WERE LADY JANE AND INCAS?

INCAS WAS A MALE CAROLINA PARAKEET LIVING IN THE FORESTS OF THE SOUTHERN UNITED STATES IN THE LATE 1800S.

WHEN INCAS WAS VERY YOUNG HE WAS CAPTURED WHILE PERCHING QUIETLY WITH HIS FLOCK.

INCAS WAS TAKEN TO CINCINNATI ZOO AND PUT IN A CAGE. THERE HE MET LADY JANE, ANOTHER YOUNG CAROLINA PARAKEET.

INCAS AND LADY JANE FELL HEAD OVER CLAWS IN LOVE, AND SHARED THEIR CAGE AND FOOD FOR SEVERAL YEARS.

ONE DAY LADY JANE DIED, LEAVING INCAS HEARTBROKEN. A FEW MONTHS LATER, CONSUMED BY GRIEF, INCAS JOINED HER IN DEATH.

THAT WAS IN 1918. LADY JANE AND INCAS ARE NOW KNOWN TO HAVE BEEN THE VERY LAST CAROLINA PARAKEETS.

THE CAROLINA PARAKEET

CONUROPSIS CAROLINENSIS

SIZE: 1 to 1 foot 2 inches long
WEIGHT: 1/3 of an ounce
FOUND IN: Southeastern
United States
DATE OF EXTINCTION:
1918

Just like the passenger pigeon, the **Carolina parakeet** suffered a terrible fate. In one century, its numbers fell from several million to just a few birds, then the species vanished altogether. Its extinction was partly the result of trapping by humans, who saw it as a pest because it fed on crops and orchard fruit. The parrots' idiosyncratic behavior made them easy prey. They would never abandon a wounded member of their flock. When one bird was hit, the others would stay perched nearby, making them easy targets.

A set routine
Carolina parakeets were active at sunrise and sunset. During the day, they rested.

A very sociable bird
Carolina parakeets traveled in flocks of 100 to 1,000 birds. They were very attached to their flying companions and could not live alone.

A splash of color
Like many other parrots, the Carolina parakeet had brightly colored feathers. Its body was vivid green and its head was yellow and orange.

WHO WAS NICKNAMED "LONESOME GEORGE"?

IN 1971, A SCIENTIST DISCOVERED A MALE GIANT TORTOISE THAT WOULD SOON HIT HEADLINES AROUND THE WORLD. THE SCIENTIST WAS WANDERING AROUND ON PINTA ISLAND IN THE GALAPAGOS WHEN HE CAME UPON THE TORTOISE DESTINED TO BE CALLED "LONESOME GEORGE." PEOPLE SEARCHED THE WHOLE ISLAND, BUT GEORGE WAS THE ONLY ONE.

LONESOME GEORGE QUICKLY BECAME A GLOBAL CELEBRITY. AS THE LAST REMAINING PINTA ISLAND TORTOISE, HE WAS UNIQUE. SCIENTISTS TOLD THE WORLD ABOUT HIM AND MADE IT CLEAR THERE WAS NO TIME TO LOSE IN SAVING OTHER ANIMALS IN THE AREA.

SCIENTISTS BROUGHT OTHER TORTOISES TO GEORGE'S ISLAND TO TRY TO GIVE HIS SPECIES A FUTURE. THEY INTRODUCED HIM TO SEVERAL PRETTY, FRIENDLY FEMALES, BUT GEORGE HAD LIVED ALONE FOR TOO LONG AND COULDN'T MUSTER MUCH INTEREST. HOWEVER, AFTER THINKING ABOUT IT FOR 34 YEARS, GEORGE FINALLY GAVE IN AND MATED. IF HE BECOMES A DAD, THE SPECIES MIGHT JUST SURVIVE...

THE LONESOME TORTOISE OF PINTA ISLAND

GEOCHELONE NIGRA ABINGDONI

SIZE: 4 feet long
WEIGHT: 198 pounds
FOUND IN: Pinta Island
DATE OF EXTINCTION:
As far away as
possible.

George is a member of the species known collectively as **Galapagos tortoises**. It contains several subspecies that live on small islands, and each has distinctive traits. These tortoises had a peaceful life until the Galapagos archipelago was discovered in the 1500s. Then they were slaughtered by European sailors and harmed by introduced animals like goats, which ate their food. Their numbers fell dramatically and some subspecies were wiped out. Today, the last members of this critically endangered species are closely monitored.

Quite a bite!
Although toothless, George has a sharp beak he uses to chomp on plants and fruit, his staple diet.

Islands of oldies
George is about 100 years old and still in good health. But that isn't old for a Galapagos tortoise. One of his relatives, Harriet, lived to 176!

A protective shell
Like his male and female relatives on other islands, George has a solid shell. When he feels threatened, he pulls his head inside.

AFRICA

The African zone takes in the continent of Africa, from the Atlas
Mountains to the southernmost tip of South Africa, and the Indian Ocean
islands, including Madagascar.

There are more than 3,000 islands in the Indian Ocean. Most were
discovered relatively recently. The arrival of Westerners in the 1500s led
to the disappearance of several animals, including the dodo of Mauritius
and the elephant bird of Madagascar.

Africa is now home to several endangered animals
including the elephant, the lion, and the gorilla.
Although awareness is growing about the need to
protect them, these animals are still hunted.

IS THE TERRIBLE KILOPILOPITSOFY STILL HAUNTING MADAGASCAR'S FORESTS?

MADAGASCAR IS RICH IN FOLK TALES. IT'S SAID THAT ITS FORESTS ARE HAUNTED BY MONSTERS. ONE OF THESE BEASTS IS THE KIDOKY, A GIANT LEMUR WITH A HUMAN FACE. ANOTHER IS THE BOKYBOKY, A SMALL MAMMAL WITH STRIPED FUR, SUPPOSED TO HAVE MAGICAL POWERS.

BUT ONE CREATURE ON THE ISLAND IS PARTICULARLY TERRIFYING. IT IS SAID TO ONLY COME OUT AT NIGHT. IT'S THE SIZE OF A CALF, WITH DARK SKIN AND A GREAT MOUTHFUL OF LONG TEETH, AND IT MAKES A DISTINCTIVE GRUNTING SOUND. MALAGASY PEOPLE CALL THIS BEAST THE "KILOPILOPITSOFY" AND MANY FEAR IT WILL CATCH THEM AND GOBBLE THEM UP.

IN FACT, SEVERAL PIECES OF RESEARCH INTO THE INFAMOUS "KILOPILOPITSOFY" HAVE CONCLUDED THAT IT WAS PROBABLY NOT VERY DANGEROUS: EYEWITNESS ACCOUNTS EVEN SUGGEST THAT THIS "BEAST" WAS THE SPITTING IMAGE OF ... A DWARF HIPPOPOTAMUS! RESEARCH ALSO SUGGESTS THAT THIS ANIMAL DIED OUT LONG AGO. HAVE THE MALAGASY PEOPLE BEEN SCARED OF A GHOST?

THE MALAGASY DWARF HIPPOPOTAMUS

HIPPOPOTAMUS LEMERLEI

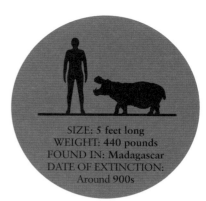

SIZE: 5 feet long
WEIGHT: 440 pounds
FOUND IN: Madagascar
DATE OF EXTINCTION:
Around 900s

The Malagasy **dwarf hippopotamus** is thought to have disappeared a very long time ago. However, its most recent remains are less than 500 years old. Some people believe it was still alive in isolated parts of the island in recent centuries. This hippopotamus lives on in Malagasy legend and inspired the monster known as the kilopilopitsofy, which still haunts the forests of Madagascar.

37

WAS THE GIANT ROC A GOOD WAY TO TRAVEL?

SINBAD THE SAILOR IS A HERO WHOSE ADVENTURES ARE TOLD IN THE BOOK, *ONE THOUSAND AND ONE NIGHTS*. ON HIS SECOND VOYAGE, SINBAD FINDS HIMSELF STRANDED ALONE ON A DESERT ISLAND.

JUST WHEN HE THINKS ALL IS LOST, HE SEES A STRANGE WHITE OBJECT IN THE DISTANCE. HE IS AMAZED TO FIND IT HAS NO KIND OF OPENING. IT'S LIKE NOTHING HE'S EVER SEEN.

SUDDENLY THE SKY TURNS DARK. LOOKING UP, SINBAD SEES A HUGE BIRD FLYING STRAIGHT FOR HIM. THE MYSTERIOUS WHITE BOULDER MUST BE ITS EGG.

THE GIANT BIRD LANDS NEAR THE EGG, WHILE SINBAD TUCKS HIMSELF BEHIND IT. HE REMEMBERS OTHER SAILORS SPEAKING OF AN EXTRAORDINARY BIRD CALLED A ROC. MIGHT IT REALLY EXIST?

WITH THE BIRD'S FOOT SO CLOSE, SINBAD DECIDES TO BENEFIT FROM HIS TERRIFYING ENCOUNTER AND FLEE THE ISLAND. HE UNRAVELS HIS TURBAN AND STRAPS HIMSELF TO THE BIRD. AFTER A LONG WAIT, IT FINALLY TAKES OFF.

THE ROC SOARS AWAY FROM THE ISLAND AND LANDS IN A DEEP VALLEY. SINBAD QUICKLY UNTIES HIMSELF. TO HIS ASTONISHMENT, HE SEES THE GROUND IS STREWN WITH DIAMONDS. HIS NEXT ADVENTURE HAS JUST BEGUN...

THE ELEPHANT BIRD

AEPYORNIS MAXIMUS

When fossilized bones and eggs from **Aepyornis** were discovered in the 1800s, many people thought that this enormous bird from Madagascar must have been the inspiration for the legendary roc. Its size would have made an impression on sailors who landed on the island—a bird large enough to carry a man as it flew! Today we know that that's very unlikely: *Aepyornis* was a ratite, a kind of giant flightless ostrich. Known also as the elephant bird, it disappeared in the 1600s.

SIZE: 10 feet tall
WEIGHT: 1000 pounds
FOUND IN: Madagascar
DATE OF EXTINCTION:
Early 1600s

A running bird
With its small, stumpy wings, the *Aepyornis* could not fly. However, its strong three-toed feet were ideal for running.

The legend of the vorompatra
According to local stories, a giant bird known as the vorompatra lived in the swamps of Madagascar until the end of the 1800s. Given the descriptions, it seems it could have been the *Aepyornis*, which might have survived for longer than we think.

Giant eggs
The eggs laid by *Aepyornis* weren't as enormous as in Sinbad's story, but they were still very big—the equivalent of about 100 hen's eggs!

HOW DID POOR OLD ITOVO BECOME A GIANT LEMUR?

THE PEOPLE OF MADAGASCAR HAVE AN UNUSUAL RELATIONSHIP WITH LEMURS. LEGEND HAS IT THAT THESE ANIMALS ARE MEN WHO LONG AGO LOST THEIR HUMAN FORM.

THE STORY OF ITOVO EXPLAINS ONE OF THESE MAGICAL TRANSFORMATIONS. ITOVO WAS A HUMBLE FARMER MARRIED TO A RICH BUT QUARRELSOME WOMAN.

THE VILLAGE WITCH DOCTOR GAVE ITOVO A GRAVE WARNING— HE MUST NEVER TOUCH THE BIG WOODEN RICE-SERVING SPOON AT THE SAME TIME AS HIS WIFE.

MONTHS PASSED, THEN ITOVO AND HIS WIFE BEGAN TO QUARREL. DURING ONE ARGUMENT, SHE HIT HIM WITH THE BIG WOODEN SPOON.

ITOVO WAS POWERLESS TO STOP THE CURSE. HE TURNED INTO A GIANT LEMUR, THEN FLED INTO THE FOREST AND NEVER CAME BACK.

IT'S SAID THAT ITOVO'S LEMUR OFFSPRING HAVE HATED WOMEN EVER SINCE AND NEVER MISS A CHANCE TO PINCH THEM WHEN THEY'RE OUT WALKING IN THE FOREST.

THE TRATRATRATRA

PALAEOPROPITHECUS

SIZE: 5 feet tall
WEIGHT: 110 to 175 pounds
FOUND IN: Madagascar
DATE OF EXTINCTION:
About 1500

Giant lemurs like *Palaeopropithecus*, *Megaladapis* and *Archaeolemur* didn't survive long once humans came to Madagascar. However, they are the subject of several folk tales that claim they are descended from humans. They do look unsettlingly human—their posture, their grasping hands, and even their faces and expressions led the Malagasy people to believe these lemurs were able to think like people. There are still lemurs alive today that are descended from these giants. They feature heavily in Malagasy legends, and some are even treated as sacred.

A startling nickname
The tratratratra (or tretretretre) is the name given to the giant lemur by the Malagasy, the people of Madagascar.

Who's scared of whom?
The tratratratra was a solitary animal, feared by the Malagasy. But the lemur was scared of humans, too, and would swing away into the trees when it saw them.

WHO SAVED THE TAMBALACOQUE TREE?

THE TAMBALACOQUE TREE GROWS ONLY ON MAURITIUS, AN ISLAND NEAR MADAGASCAR. IT CAN GROW UP TO 65 FEET TALL, WITH A BROAD TRUNK AND DEEP ROOTS THAT MAKE IT VERY HARDY.

IN THE 1970S, PEOPLE NOTICED THAT THE TREE WAS DYING OUT. THE FEW REMAINING SPECIMENS WERE OVER 300 YEARS OLD. NO YOUNGER TREES WERE GROWING.

ONE RESEARCHER HAD A THEORY: THE TREES BEGAN TO DISAPPEAR AT ABOUT THE SAME TIME AS THE ILLUSTRIOUS BIRD, THE DODO, DIED OUT IN THE LATE 1600S.

THE LINK IS INTRIGUING! WHEN THE DODO ATE AND DIGESTED THE TREES' SEEDS, THEY WERE FREED FROM THEIR THICK, HARD SHELLS. THIS ALLOWED THE SEEDS TO GERMINATE, CREATING MORE TREES.

TO SAVE THE TAMBALACOQUE, THE EXTINCT DODO WAS REPLACED WITH THE WILD TURKEY, WHICH HAS A SIMILAR DIGESTIVE SYSTEM. THE RESULTS WERE CONVINCING: SEVERAL SEEDS GERMINATED.

TODAY THERE'S SOME DOUBT SURROUNDING THIS THEORY ABOUT THE SYMBIOTIC RELATIONSHIP BETWEEN THE TREE AND THE DODO. BUT IT IS STILL OFTEN CITED AS AN EXAMPLE OF HOW LIVING THINGS DEPEND ON EACH OTHER, AND HOW HUMANS CAN INFLUENCE THIS BALANCE...

THE DODO
RAPHUS CUCULLATUS

The **dodo** was a flightless bird related to the pigeon. It had no predators until Europeans came to Mauritius. Because it was so heavy, the plump dodo was a clumsy mover and could not fly. Such easy prey was very quickly wiped out. The Dutch killed and ate dodos in the greatest numbers. Introduced animals—including cats, goats, feral dogs, and pigs, along with rats which ate the dodos' eggs—drove the bird to extinction sometime around 1680.

SIZE: 2 feet 7 inches tall
WEIGHT: 44 pounds
FOUND IN: Mauritius
DATE OF EXTINCTION:
Before 1700

An extinct star
In the 1800s, the dodo was simply a strange creature that had all but disappeared from memory. When Lewis Carroll made the dodo a character in his book *Alice's Adventures in Wonderland*, it became famous and still fascinates today. Many people think the dodo is imaginary, but it was once very much alive.

An odd name
"Dodo" comes from the Portuguese *doido* which means "crazy" or "stupid," and the Dutch *dodars* or *dodoors* which means "lazy."

An Egyptian-style nest
The dodo built its unusual pyramid-shaped nest from palm leaves, straight on the ground.

EURASIA

Eurasia is a supercontinent in the northern hemisphere. It is bordered by the Atlantic Ocean to the west, the Arctic to the north, the Mediterranean and Indian Oceans to the south, and the Pacific Ocean to the east.

The islands of the Mediterranean have been home to several dwarf and giant animals that are now extinct. Some inspired Greek and Roman myths.

Throughout the 1900s, the continent became industrialized. Pollution and habitat loss have been increasingly threatening to animals and plants. The Bali tiger and the Chinese river dolphin are two of the best-known recent extinctions in Asia.

WHO WON THE INTERNATIONAL ANTLER CONTEST?

SPECIES OF DEER ARE FOUND ALL OVER THE WORLD. MOST OF THEM HAVE ANTLERS: BONY, BRANCHED GROWTHS ON THEIR HEADS.

IT'S USUALLY MALE DEER THAT HAVE ANTLERS, AND THEY USE THEM TO IMPRESS AND WOO THE FEMALES. UNLIKE HORNS, ANTLERS FALL OFF AND GROW BACK EVERY YEAR.

THE DEER FAMILY IS HUGELY VARIED, AND SO ARE THE ANTLERS OF EACH SPECIES. THE SMALLEST DEER, THE SOUTHERN PUDU, HAS SHORT, POINTED ANTLERS.

ITS COUSIN, THE EUROPEAN ROE DEER, IS ONLY SLIGHTLY TALLER AND ALSO HAS SHORT ANTLERS. THE RED DEER, HOWEVER, IS ONE OF THE LARGER SPECIES: ITS ANTLERS ARE FAR MORE IMPRESSIVE.

THE REINDEER (PICTURED IN THE TOP RIGHT FRAME) LIVES IN NORTHERN EUROPE AND AMERICA, AND HAS LONG, SLENDER ANTLERS. THE MOOSE (IN THIS CARTOON) IS THE LARGEST LIVING MEMBER OF THE DEER FAMILY. HE HAS DISTINCTIVE FLAT, BRANCHED ANTLERS.

BUT NONE COME CLOSE TO THE IRISH ELK—ITS HUGE ANTLERS COULD GROW TO MORE THAN TEN FEET FROM BASE TO TIP. IT WOULD HAVE WON THE INTERNATIONAL ANTLER CONTEST FOR SURE!

THE IRISH ELK

MEGALOCEROS GIGANTEUS

The **Megaloceros** was one of the largest deer that ever lived. It was found in the damp, cold plains of northern Europe and Asia. For a long time it was thought that its height and huge antlers caused it to die out. In fact, about 15,000 years ago, after a dramatic change in climate, forests began to spring up where it lived. Its massive antlers kept it from moving freely in this new environment and made it easy prey for the European cave lion, Neanderthal man, and our immediate ancestor, *Homo sapiens*.

SIZE: 7 feet tall
WEIGHT: 550 pounds
FOUND IN: Europe and Asia
DATE OF EXTINCTION:
10,000 years ago

Awkward antlers
Megaloceros antlers were about ten feet wide and weighed more than 65 pounds. They fell off and regrew every year, just like those of deer and elk today.

Why Irish?
Megaloceros is called the Irish elk (and the "peat-bog deer" in French) because so many of its bones have been found in Ireland's bogs. These remains have allowed scientists to learn more about the animal.

The last survivors
The remains of several Irish elk were recently found on an island near Scotland. They were dated to only 7,500 BC. Scientists concluded that a small herd had managed to survive in this isolated spot.

WHAT IS SIBERIA'S LARGEST TREASURE?

SIBERIA IS A REGION IN THE FAR NORTH OF RUSSIA. THANKS TO ITS EXTREME TEMPERATURES, IT IS HOME TO UNTOLD NATURAL TREASURES. IN 1997, AFTER A TIP-OFF FROM A GROUP OF HUNTERS, SOME SCIENTISTS SET OUT TO FIND ONE OF THEM.

WHEN THEY GOT TO THE RIGHT SPOT, THE SCIENTISTS UNCOVERED TWO VERY LONG, INTACT MAMMOTH TUSKS. BUT WHAT THEY FOUND WHEN THEY DUG DEEPER WAS BEYOND THEIR WILDEST DREAMS—BENEATH THE TUSKS WAS AN ANIMAL NEARLY 20,000 YEARS OLD AND PRACTICALLY STILL IN ONE PIECE.

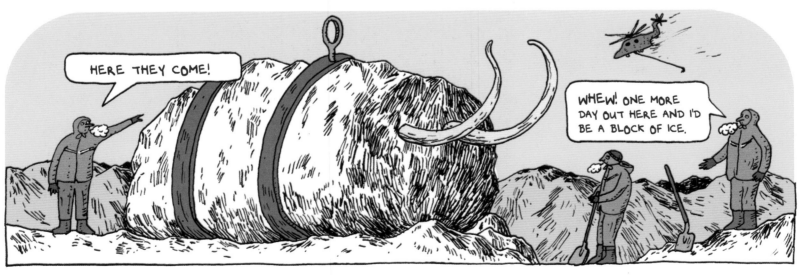

THEY SPENT MONTHS CAREFULLY DIGGING IT OUT. THEN THE PREHISTORIC MAMMOTH WAS LIFTED BY THE WORLD'S BIGGEST HELICOPTER AND TAKEN IN ITS ICY COFFIN TO A LABORATORY WHERE SCIENTISTS SLOWLY DEFROSTED AND STUDIED IT OVER SEVERAL YEARS.

THE WOOLLY MAMMOTH

MAMMUTHUS PRIMIGENIUS

SIZE: 13 feet tall
WEIGHT: 6.6 to 11 tons
FOUND IN: Siberia
DATE OF EXTINCTION:
10,000 years ago

The **mammoth** is an ancient animal that was able to adapt to periods of climate change by altering the length of its hair. About 15,000 years ago, there was a rapid temperature rise. The vast grassy plains where it lived were transformed into pine forest. The herbivorous mammoth couldn't adapt to a new diet and became weak. It is likely that hunting also hastened its extinction.

She's the boss
Woolly mammoths probably lived in matriarchal groups, like modern-day elephants. The oldest female was the head of the group.

Handy tusks...
Woolly mammoths had long, curved tusks which they used in battle, for show, and for gathering vegetation to eat.

...and long hair
This animal is described as "woolly" because of its thick winter coat which grew up to three feet long—good insulation against the bitter Siberian cold.

Did hercules skin the last european lion?

IN ANCIENT TIMES, A HUGE LION TOOK UP RESIDENCE IN THE FORESTS OF NEMEA, IN GREECE. MEN AND ANIMALS WERE TERRIFIED OF IT.

THE FIRST OF THE HERO HERCULES' TWELVE TASKS WAS TO KILL THE LION. HERCULES VENTURED INTO THE FOREST IN SEARCH OF HIS FORMIDABLE PREY.

FINALLY HE SPOTTED THE FAMOUS NEMEAN LION. HE FIRED AT IT WITH DEADLY ARROWS—BUT THEY BOUNCED OFF ITS SKIN, LEAVING NOT A SCRATCH.

HERCULES WAS UNDETERRED, AND WITH A GREAT YELL SWUNG HIS CLUB AND SMASHED IT DOWN ON THE LION'S HEAD.

THE CLUB SHATTERED. THE ANIMAL WAS STUNNED. HERCULES TOOK HIS CHANCE TO GRAB THE LION AND SQUEEZE ITS NECK WITH ALL HIS MIGHT TO STRANGLE IT.

TO PROVE HE'D COMPLETED HIS TASK, HERCULES CUT UP THE LION AND MADE A CLOAK FROM ITS SKIN. LEGEND HAS IT THAT THE SKIN WAS SO TOUGH HE COULD WEAR IT AS ARMOR.

THE EUROPEAN LION

PANTHERA LEO EUROPAEA

The **European lion** is a subspecies of lion that lived in ancient times. It inspired legends like the one about Hercules fighting the Nemean lion. It disappeared due to the spread of the Greek and Roman civilizations in the Mediterranean. It was likely hunted to stop it attacking flocks, but it might also have been used in religious sacrifices. Also, the popular animal fights—held in Roman arenas—where hundreds of big cats were slaughtered, seem likely to have wiped out the few remaining lions.

SIZE: 4 feet tall
WEIGHT: 440 pounds
FOUND IN: Mediterranean countries
DATE OF EXTINCTION: About AD 100

A small lion
The European lion was smaller and lighter than the African lion, and its mane wasn't as thick.

A home in the forest
The African lion lives in the savannah, but its European cousin preferred the forest.

A cousin in the mountains
The European lion had a relative in the Atlas Mountains in Africa. Although a few of these Atlas lions still exist, none have lived in the wild for half a century.

WHAT'S THE LINK BETWEEN A CYCLOPS AND A DWARF ELEPHANT?

SICILY, AN ISLAND IN SOUTHERN ITALY, IS A LAND OF LEGENDS. IT IS SAID THAT HEPHAESTUS, THE BLACKSMITH GOD, HAD HIS FORGE AT THE FOOT OF MOUNT ETNA WHERE HELIOS, THE SUN GOD, GRAZED HIS SHEEP.

THE ISLAND WAS ALSO SAID TO BE HOME TO TERRIFYING MONSTERS WITH A SINGLE EYE IN THE MIDDLE OF THE FOREHEAD—THE CYCLOPS. THEY APPEARED TO LIVE AS PEACEFUL SHEPHERDS BUT WERE IN FACT FEARSOME MAN-EATERS.

THE HERO ODYSSEUS MET THEM ON HIS ODYSSEY. HE WANTED TO FIND OUT MORE ABOUT THESE SAVAGE GIANTS, BUT HE AND HIS COMPANIONS WERE CAPTURED BY A CYCLOPS NAMED POLYPHEMUS.

IF I CATCH YOU, MY VENGEANCE WILL BE TERRIBLE!

ODYSSEUS USED TRICKERY TO ESCAPE THE CYCLOPS' CLUTCHES. HELD PRISONER IN A CAVE, ODYSSEUS GOT POLYPHEMUS DRUNK THEN STABBED HIM IN THE EYE. HE AND HIS FRIENDS THEN ESCAPED BY CLINGING TO THE BELLIES OF SHEEP.

STOP!

BUT WHERE DID THE GREEK AND ROMAN STORIES ABOUT THE CYCLOPS COME FROM? IN THE 1800s, SCIENTISTS DUG UP SKULLS THAT MAY EXPLAIN THEIR ORIGINS.

?

WELL, UH, YOU WERE ABOUT TO SQUISH ME.

THESE SKULLS WERE ACTUALLY FROM DWARF ELEPHANTS THAT HAD BEEN LIVING ON THE ISLAND FOR A VERY LONG TIME. PEOPLE MAY HAVE COME TO BELIEVE IN THE CYCLOPS BECAUSE THEY MISTOOK THE NASAL HOLE IN THE ELEPHANT'S SKULL (WHERE ITS TRUNK CAME OUT) FOR A SINGLE EYE SOCKET.

THE SICILIAN DWARF ELEPHANT

ELEPHAS FALCONERI

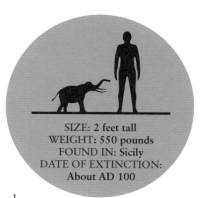

SIZE: 2 feet tall
WEIGHT: 550 pounds
FOUND IN: Sicily
DATE OF EXTINCTION:
About AD 100

More than 12,000 years ago there were dwarf elephants on most Mediterranean islands, including Sicily, Malta, Sardinia, Cyprus, and Crete. They had either swum or come overland from Europe, depending on sea levels. Since they had no predators on these islands, they evolved to an unusually small size. The woodland elephant, their European ancestor, was more than ten feet tall but the island-dwelling dwarf elephants didn't even reach three feet. Of them all, the **Sicilian dwarf elephant** survived the longest—until Roman times.

WHO WERE THE INVINCIBLE AUROCHS?

THE FIRST CATTLE BEAST KNOWN TO MAN WAS THE AUROCHS, A WILD ANIMAL DEPICTED IN ROCK PAINTINGS, SUCH AS THOSE IN THE LASCAUX CAVES IN FRANCE. IN THESE PREHISTORIC FRESCOES, THE AUROCHS LOOKS ENORMOUS. ITS SIZE AND STRENGTH MUST HAVE MADE A GREAT IMPRESSION ON ANCIENT HUNTERS.

IN TIME, MEN BECAME VERY SKILLED AT HUNTING THE AUROCHS AND LEARNED TO RAISE THEIR OWN HERDS. THIS EARLY DOMESTICATION BEGAN ABOUT 8,000 YEARS AGO IN THE MIDDLE EAST, THEN SPREAD TO INDIA AND EUROPE. ALL DOMESTIC CATTLE (FROM THE EUROPEAN BULL TO THE INDIAN ZEBU) ARE DESCENDED FROM THE AUROCHS.

NOT ALL AUROCHS WERE DOMESTICATED. A FEW REBELS REMAINED WILD. BUT THEIR ONCE VAST TERRITORY SHRANK AND THEY WERE HARDLY SEEN IN EUROPE AFTER ROMAN TIMES. THE AUROCHS WERE HUNTED AND DRIVEN INTO EVER SMALLER POCKETS OF FOREST. THE LAST FEW DIED IN POLAND IN 1627.

THE AUROCHS
BOS PRIMIGENIUS

Once there were three subspecies of **aurochs** from three different places: ***Bos primigenius*** from Asia, ***Bos primigenius africanus*** from North Africa, and ***Bos primigenius primigenius*** from Europe and the Middle East. The latter survived until the Middle Ages in the great forests of Europe. Its predators were wolves and humans. Intensive hunting and disappearing habitat finally made it extinct.

SIZE: 6 feet 6 inches tall
WEIGHT: 1 ton
FOUND IN: From India to Europe
DATE OF EXTINCTION: 1627

A huge species of cattle
Aurochs looked like domestic cattle but were much bigger with a much hairier hide.

Impressive horns
Aurochs' horns were very distinctive. The male's were more than three feet wide and were formidable weapons.

Adventurous eaters
Like today's cattle, aurochs were grazers but could supplement their diet with leaves and even acorns.

WHY SHOULD THE SEA COW HAVE STAYED OUT OF SIGHT?

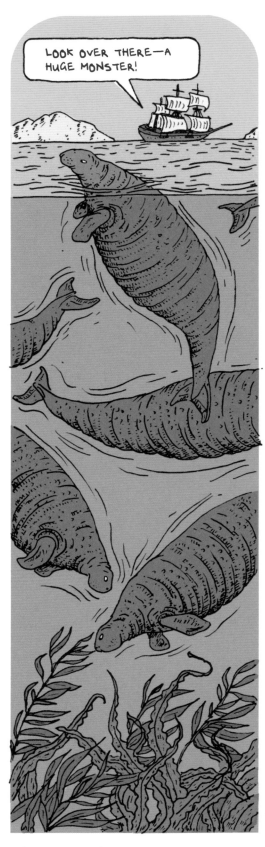

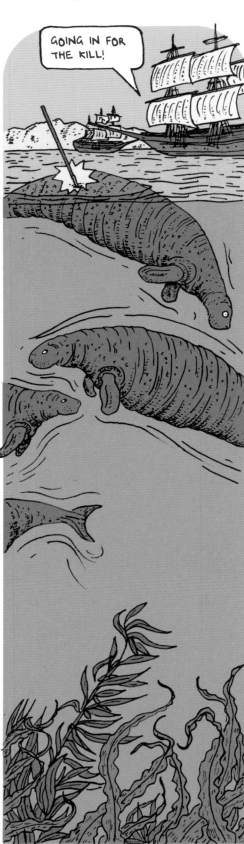

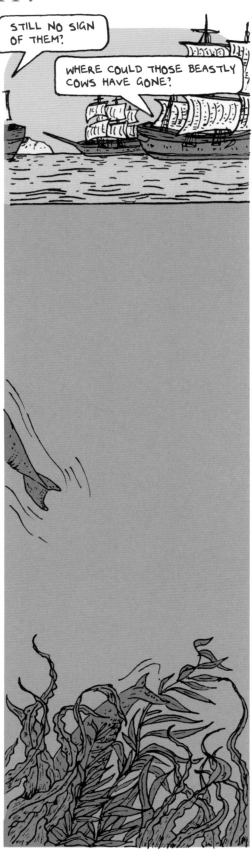

IN 1741, THE NATURALIST GEORG WILHELM STELLER DISCOVERED A STRANGE, NEW ANIMAL: THE SEA COW. (ON THE SAME EXPEDITION, VITUS BERING SAILED THROUGH THE STRAIT THAT WAS TO TAKE HIS NAME.)

THE EXPLORERS RETURNED AND COVETED THE NEW-FOUND ANIMAL. IT WAS PRIZED FOR ITS FAT, OIL, AND MEAT, AND ITS MILK WAS SAID TO BE DELICIOUS. HUNTERS AND SAILORS OF ALL SORTS WENT AFTER IT.

THE SEA COW WAS A SLOW, PLACID ANIMAL. IT WAS WIPED OUT IN RECORD TIME—LESS THAN 30 YEARS AFTER IT WAS DISCOVERED IT WAS DECLARED EXTINCT. CLAIMS OF SIGHTINGS HAVE BEEN MADE SINCE THEN, BUT WITHOUT EVIDENCE.

STELLER'S SEA COW

HYDRODAMALIS GIGAS

More than 10,000 years ago, **Steller's sea cow** lived in various parts of the
North Pacific, from Japan up to the Gulf of Alaska. When it was first sighted
in the 1700s, it had already retreated to a small area near the Bering Strait,
which humans hadn't yet discovered. The 2,000 sea cows living there were
thoughtlessly slaughtered and the species was quickly wiped out.

SIZE: 26 feet long
WEIGHT: 6.6 tons
FOUND IN: The Arctic
DATE OF EXTINCTION:
1768

A wrinkly mammal
The sea cow's skin was very thick and covered in
wrinkles, which is how it got its earlier scientific
name, *Rhytina stelleri* ("rhytina" comes from a
Greek word meaning fold or wrinkle).

An underwater grazer
It had no teeth. Instead it had
two large horny plates with
which to grind up kelp.

An underwater cow
The sea cow lived in herds and spent
most of its time nibbling on kelp. It's not
surprising it got its name!

ARE TIGERS DOOMED TO DISAPPEAR?

IN ASIA, TIGER HUNTING IS AN ANCIENT TRADITION. TO TAKE ON AND KILL SUCH A WILD ANIMAL IS CONSIDERED BY SOME TO BE A DANGEROUS AND COURAGEOUS FEAT. IN INDIA, IT USED TO BE THE MAHARAJAHS' FAVORITE PASTIME, AND THEY ORGANIZED HUNTING EXPEDITIONS ON ELEPHANT AND HORSEBACK.

WHEN EUROPEAN COLONISTS ARRIVED WITH GUNS IN THE 1500S, THE TRADITIONAL HUNTS BECAME BLOODBATHS. THE CARNAGE INCREASED IN THE 1900S AND LED TO THE DISAPPEARANCE OF ALL TIGERS ON THE ISLANDS OF BALI AND JAVA.

IN LESS THAN A CENTURY, THE TOTAL NUMBER OF TIGERS LIVING IN THE WILD FELL FROM 100,000 TO FEWER THAN 4,000. ALTHOUGH WILDLIFE PROTECTION LAWS HAVE BEEN PASSED IN RECENT DECADES, THE TIGER IS NOW AT SERIOUS RISK OF EXTINCTION. ITS HABITAT IS SHRINKING THROUGH DEFORESTATION, AND POACHERS STILL HUNT IT FOR ITS SKIN AND ORGANS, WHICH ARE PRIZED IN CHINESE MEDICINE.

THE BALI TIGER
PANTHERA TIGRIS BALICA

The **Bali tiger** is one of nine subspecies of tiger, three of which are now extinct. The Bali tiger lived in the forests of Bali, an island in Indonesia. It disappeared as a result of habitat destruction and hunting. Balinese people didn't hunt tigers because they were afraid of them—tigers were thought to embody both protective and evil powers. In the 1800s and 1900s, when European settlers arrived and began hunting the tiger, its numbers plummeted. By 1937, it had vanished. The aim of these hunts was to kill the animal for personal glory, and the tiger had little hope of survival.

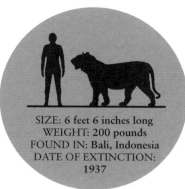

SIZE: 6 feet 6 inches long
WEIGHT: 200 pounds
FOUND IN: Bali, Indonesia
DATE OF EXTINCTION:
1937

59

WHEN DID THE CHINESE RIVER DOLPHIN OFFICIALLY BECOME EXTINCT?

THE CHINESE RIVER DOLPHIN

LIPOTES VEXILLIFER

SIZE: 6 feet long
WEIGHT: 330 pounds
FOUND IN: China
DATE OF EXTINCTION:
2007

There are five species of freshwater dolphin. Today, two live in the Amazon and two in Asia. The fifth, the **Chinese river dolphin** which swam in the long Yangtze River, is extinct. It was famed in China, where legend says that it was the reincarnation of a Chinese princess. When the princess refused to marry against her will, her father drowned her. This is how the Chinese river dolphin, also known as the baiji, is said to have been created. In the end, industrialization and pollution got the better of this Yangtze River princess.

OCEANIA

Oceania is made up of Australia, New Zealand, and numerous islands scattered across this part of the Pacific Ocean.

Australia is a large isolated continent which is home to some very odd animals. Humans have had a hand in the extinction of many, from the giant echidna to the pig-footed bandicoot.

The islands of New Zealand, further east, remained undiscovered by humans for a very long time. Two extinct animals that once shared these islands, the moa and Haast's eagle, live on in the legends first told by the country's Māori people.

WHAT WERE AUSTRALIA'S GIANT ANIMALS?

LONG AGO, MEN CAME ASHORE ON A VAST, WILD LAND. THE ISOLATED CONTINENT WE NOW CALL AUSTRALIA WAS HOME TO SOME STRANGE CREATURES.

SOME OF THEM SEEM FAMILIAR TO US, AT FIRST. BUT ALTHOUGH THE *PROCOPTODON* LOOKED LIKE A MODERN KANGAROO, IN FACT IT WAS A SIX-FOOT-SIX-INCH-TALL GIANT.

ZAGLOSSUS HACKETTI WAS THREE FEET LONG—THREE OR FOUR TIMES BIGGER THAN THE LITTLE ECHIDNA STILL ALIVE TODAY. BUT IN MANY OTHER WAYS, THE TWO ARE SIMILAR.

THE *DIPROTODON* WAS A HULKING GREAT ANIMAL THE SIZE OF A RHINOCEROS. IT WAS THE BIGGEST MARSUPIAL THAT EVER LIVED.

IMAGINE HOW TERRIFIED AUSTRALIA'S FIRST INHABITANTS MUST HAVE BEEN WHEN THEY FIRST SPOTTED THE 26-FOOT-LONG GIANT LIZARD *MEGALANIA PRISCA*. IT WAS A FEROCIOUS PREDATOR.

THERE WERE FEARSOME CARNIVORES LIVING IN THIS UNEXPLORED LAND. THE MARSUPIAL LION (*THYLACOLEO*) AND THE THYLACINE (SEE PAGE 71) WERE SMALL BUT FORMIDABLE HUNTERS.

THE LONG-BEAKED ECHIDNA

ZAGLOSSUS HACKETTI

Zaglossus hacketti, or the **long-beaked echidna**, belongs to the group of unusual giant animals (also called "megafauna") that roamed the Australian continent about 40,000 years ago, when humans first arrived in this unexplored land. These animals gradually died out as a result of climate change, many of them 15,000 years ago. According to some theories, humans played a role in their demise—as soon as humans arrived, they relentlessly hunted these animals and lit fires that destroyed their habitat.

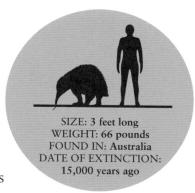

SIZE: 3 feet long
WEIGHT: 66 pounds
FOUND IN: Australia
DATE OF EXTINCTION:
15,000 years ago

What's a monotreme?
The echidna is very unusual. Like the platypus, it is a monotreme—an animal which is both oviparous (it lays eggs), and also a mammal (it produces milk for its young).

A huge hedgehog
The long-beaked echidna looked like a hedgehog, with a long muzzle and a sticky tongue for catching insects. It was as big as a sheep.

HOW DID THE WARRIOR RURU CONQUER THE LEGENDARY POUĀKAI?

THE POUĀKAI IS A GIANT BIRD FROM MĀORI MYTHOLOGY, WHICH SAYS THAT IT LIVED AT THE TOP OF A MOUNTAIN IN THE SOUTH ISLAND OF NEW ZEALAND.

THE HUGE BIRD WOULD SPOT ITS PREY FROM ITS NEST. ITS SIZE AND SPEED MADE IT THE ISLAND'S TOP PREDATOR.

ITS FAVORITE PREY WAS THE MOA, BUT THE POUĀKAI WAS ALSO REPUTED TO CARRY OFF MEN TO FEED ON.

RURU, A FAMOUS BIRD-HUNTER, LED AN EXPEDITION TO KILL THE POUĀKAI. BUT BECAUSE THE BIRD WAS TOO POWERFUL TO ATTACK HEAD-ON, THEY SET A TRAP INSTEAD.

RURU AND FIVE OTHER MEMBERS OF HIS TRIBE WOVE A NET AND SUBMERGED IT IN A LAKE NEAR THE MOUNTAIN. THE HUNTERS HID UNDER THE NET AND RURU CALLED THE BIRD.

WHEN IT TRIED TO ATTACK, THE BIRD'S FEET WERE CAUGHT IN THE NET. THE HUNTERS PULLED IT INTO THE WATER. WITHOUT ITS FEARSOME CLAWS FOR DEFENCE, THE POUĀKAI WAS SWIFTLY KILLED BY THE HUNTERS.

HAAST'S EAGLE

HARPAGORNIS MOOREI

More than 500 years ago, a huge eagle with a wingspan of ten feet—**Haast's eagle**—ruled the forests of New Zealand. Research has shown that it became so enormous because it had no terrestrial predators and fed on large animals. Haast's eagle grew so big it pushed the physical boundaries of flight for a bird of prey. Some scientists think it died out with no help from humans—certain subspecies of moa on which it fed became scarce, so it may not have survived anyway.

SIZE: 10 foot wingspan
WEIGHT: 33 pounds
FOUND IN: New Zealand
DATE OF EXTINCTION:
About 1400

A formidable hunter
Haast's eagle probably lived in the forest, sighting its prey from the treetops, and swooping down on it at more than 50 miles per hour. The prey would have been stunned by the impact and quickly killed by the eagle's sharp talons.

Tiger's claws
Larger than any eagle alive today, it had strong feet and talons resembling a tiger's claws.

WHO WERE THE "MOA HUNTERS"?

NEW ZEALAND IS VERY YOUNG IN TERMS OF HUMAN HISTORY—ITS FIRST INHABITANTS ARRIVED IN OCEAN-GOING CANOES AROUND A THOUSAND YEARS AGO. THESE POLYNESIANS FROM OTHER PACIFIC ISLANDS VENTURED ASHORE ON THIS UNKNOWN LAND, AFTER PADDLING FOR WEEKS OR MONTHS. THEY CAME TO BE CALLED THE MĀORI.

THE MOST COMMON CREATURES IN THIS NEW LAND WERE BIRDS. SOME OF THEM WERE HUGE, LIKE THE GIANT MOA WHICH COULDN'T FLY AND WAS MORE THAN 10 FEET TALL. MOA WERE A WELCOME SOURCE OF FOOD FOR THE NEWLY ARRIVED MĀORI.

AT FIRST, MOA WAS A STAPLE IN THE MĀORI DIET. ITS MEAT AND EGGS WERE PLENTIFUL AND PRIZED. ITS BONES WERE USED TO MAKE TOOLS, AND ITS FEATHERS BECAME CLOTHING. IT WAS SUCH A VITAL RESOURCE FOR THE COUNTRY'S INDIGENOUS PEOPLE THAT HISTORIANS NICKNAMED THE EARLY MĀORI "MOA HUNTERS."

THE GIANT MOA
DINORNIS GIGANTEUS

The 13 known subspecies of moa lived for thousands of years on New Zealand's two main islands. The largest and most impressive was the ten-foot-tall **giant moa**—an absolute whopper of a bird. Moa disappeared more than 300 years ago, after intensive hunting by Māori. These "moa hunters" used the tactic of burning down the forests where the birds lived. The moa, whose only other predator was Haast's eagle, was no match for an enemy as destructive as man.

SIZE: **10 feet tall**
WEIGHT: **550 pounds**
FOUND IN: **New Zealand**
DATE OF EXTINCTION:
About 1700

A vegetarian bird
The moa ate leaves, twigs, and berries. Its long neck allowed it to reach food that many other animals couldn't.

A great runner
Like the ostrich, the moa was flightless. It had long, very muscular legs and razor-sharp talons.

The tallest of all time
Today the ostrich is the tallest bird in the world. Three centuries ago, the record belonged to the moa.

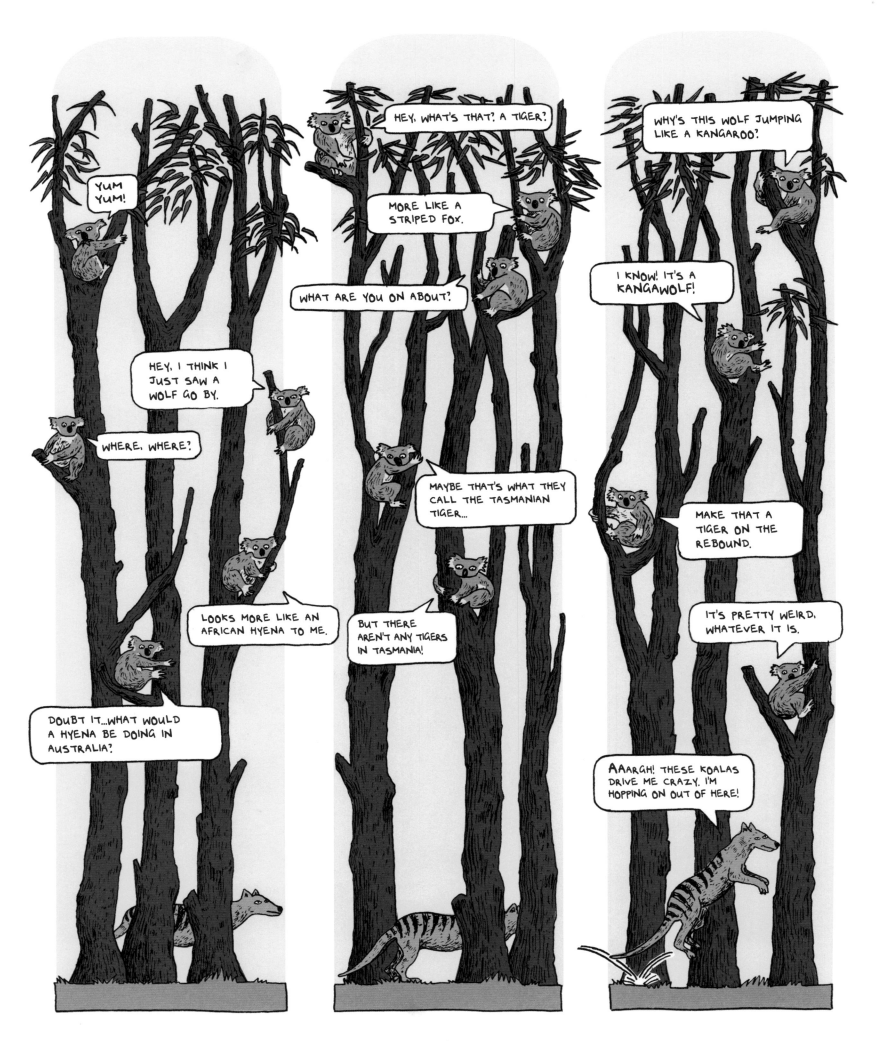

THE THYLACINE

THYLACINUS CYNOCEPHALUS

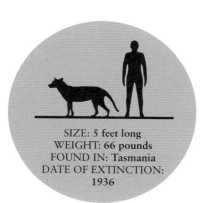

SIZE: 5 feet long
WEIGHT: 66 pounds
FOUND IN: Tasmania
DATE OF EXTINCTION:
1936

Long ago, there were **thylacines** in mainland Australia as well as on the island of Tasmania. After the first people, the Aborigines, arrived, the thylacines became extinct on the mainland. The Tasmanian thylacine lived in peace until British settlers arrived in the 1800s. These colonists decided to eradicate the animal because it attacked their cattle. They hunted it and destroyed its habitat. Despite efforts to protect it, the thylacine died out in the 1930s.

A marsupial
Although nicknamed the Tasmanian tiger or wolf, the thylacine was neither feline nor canine. In fact, it was a marsupial. Like the kangaroo, it had a pouch on its belly where it kept its babies for several months.

A strange animal
The thylacine looked like a yellowish-brown, short-haired dog. It had stripes rather like a tiger's, and a tail like a kangaroo's.

Leaps and bounds
It wasn't a fast runner, trotting with a rather clumsy gait. But it could leap like a kangaroo.

WHOSE BAD IDEA WAS IT TO BRING A PET TO AUSTRALIA?

AUSTRALIA AND NEW GUINEA ARE HOME TO SEVERAL MARSUPIALS THAT ARE FOUND NOWHERE ELSE. THESE DISTINCTIVE ANIMALS FLOURISHED FOR CENTURIES AND DEVELOPED UNUSUAL TRAITS.

WHEN EUROPEAN COLONISTS CAME TO AUSTRALIA IN THE 1700S THEY BROUGHT DOMESTIC ANIMALS WITH THEM, INCLUDING CATS, DOGS, GOATS, SHEEP, RABBITS, AND LATER, FOXES. THESE SO-CALLED INVASIVE ANIMALS WREAKED HAVOC ON THE COUNTRY'S ECOSYSTEM BECAUSE THEY ATE SO MUCH VEGETATION AND COMPETED WITH THE NATIVE ANIMALS FOR RESOURCES.

AUSTRALIA'S MARSUPIALS WERE THE INTRODUCED ANIMALS' MAIN VICTIMS. FERAL CATS AND FOXES WERE FEARSOME PREDATORS OF LITTLE BANDICOOTS AND SOME TYPES OF WALLABY. AND THE SPREAD OF DINGOES (DOMESTIC DOGS LONG AGO GONE WILD) PROBABLY PLAYED A PART IN THE EXTINCTION OF THE THYLACINE.

THE PIG-FOOTED BANDICOOT

CHAEROPUS ECAUDATUS

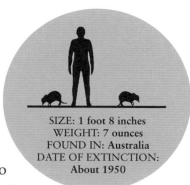

SIZE: **1 foot 8 inches**
WEIGHT: **7 ounces**
FOUND IN: **Australia**
DATE OF EXTINCTION:
About 1950

It's not known for certain why the **pig-footed bandicoot** died out, but it certainly had to do with the arrival of Europeans in Australia in the 1700s. Its disappearance was probably linked to the introduction of new animals. Rabbits and rats disturbed the local ecosystem by eating the bandicoot's food, and foxes and cats hunted and killed it.

A nap in a grassy nest
The pig-footed bandicoot was active at night. During the day, it slept in a little burrow or in a nest it made from grass.

At a gallop!
Reports of how the bandicoot moved vary. One eyewitness said it was clumsy, "like a broken-down hack." Others said it could run very fast when it had to.

A bizarre mix
The pig-footed bandicoot looked like several other animals: it had the body of a fat rat, ears like a rabbit, slender feet like an antelope, and a pig's cloven hooves.

GLOSSARY

Biodiversity

Biodiversity refers to the diversity of living things on the planet. As life has evolved on Earth there have been some periods of huge diversity and others in which a vast number of animals have disappeared, allowing new species to emerge. The periods between these two extremes have had limited diversity. Today the Earth's biodiversity is under threat. Every year, tens of thousands of species die out. Experts say we are in a period of mass extinction caused by humans.

Climate change

A climate change event (like a period of warming, or an ice age) involves a prolonged change in the planet's weather patterns. These changes affect ecosystems and have caused several species to die out. About 10,000 years ago, Earth went through several ice ages which played a part in the extinction of the **woolly mammoth** and the **giant beaver**. The climate change underway now is sure to affect the planet's biodiversity.

Dwarves and giants

Some animals evolve to be "dwarf" or "giant." Usually this happens on an island where the animal has no predators, so it's called "insular evolution." The islands of the Mediterranean were home to several dwarf animals, like the Maltese and Sicilian **dwarf elephants** which evolved from a common European ancestor ten feet tall.

Extinction

Extinction is the total disappearance of a species. It happens when the very last member of the species dies. It is difficult to know precisely when a species died out or where the last few animals were in the wild. That's why much uncertainty surrounds a species' extinction. When the last members of a species live in a zoo, we know for certain that when they die the species has disappeared. This was the case with the **Carolina parakeets** Lady Jane and Incas.

Introduced animals

Introduced animals are those brought into an ecosystem by artificial means. These animals often arrive in new places along with humans. When British settlers arrived in Australia they brought with them European animals like foxes, dogs, and cats. These animals quickly adapted to their new continent and were forced to compete with native animals, particularly marsupials like the **pig-footed bandicoot** and the **thylacine**.

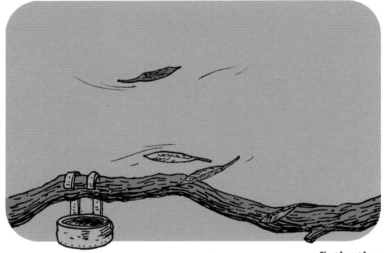

Extinction

Myths and legends

Myths and legends are ancient stories, often passed on by word of mouth, which explain the history of a place or famous person. Some tell of meetings or battles between a human and an imaginary animal. In some cases these mythical creatures are inspired by extinct animals. It's thought that the Brazilian legend of the mapinguari is based on the **giant ground sloth**, and that the famous monster kilopilopitsofy from Madagascar was in fact a **dwarf hippopotamus** which is now extinct.

Naturalist

In the 1500s, a naturalist was a scholar of natural history (botany, mineralogy or zoology). In the 1700s, the term referred to the member of a scientific expedition whose job it was to collect specimens of plants or animals. It now means someone who is a natural-history enthusiast. Naturalists like Audubon and Darwin discovered and recorded the existence of a great many animals, some of which are now extinct. Thanks to their descriptions and drawings we can still have a glimpse of them.

Myths and legends

Species

A species is a group of organisms that can interbreed and produce fertile offspring. If an isolated subset of animals from one species evolves to have distinctive characteristics it is called a "subspecies." The tiger species, for example, has nine subspecies living throughout Asia, which can be distinguished by their different sizes, weights, and coats. The Siberian tiger is the largest and can live in extreme cold. The **Bali tiger**, now extinct, was the smallest member of the species and lived on an island.

Paleontology

All sorts of creatures that once lived on Earth have left traces of themselves behind. Paleontology is the branch of science that studies these traces. By examining fossils—the remains of plants and animals preserved in rocks—paleontologists can find out how an animal lived, what it ate, and how it reproduced. The work done by the paleontologist Ameghino in South America revealed extinct animals like the **Glyptodon**.

Paleontology

Territory

This is the area in which an animal and its group lives and feeds. The bigger the animal, the larger the territory it needs, unless it can migrate. Man's territory is spreading all the time, while the space available to wild animals shrinks and fragments due to urbanization, cars and trains, dams, and power lines. This is one of the main reasons why so many animals are threatened with extinction today.

Naturalist

Pests

Pests are animals that humans consider harmful or dangerous. They often damage or destroy crops, or prey on farm animals. Labeling certain animals as pests has led to their routine extermination: that's what happened to the **passenger pigeon**, the **Carolina parakeet**, and the **Falkland Islands fox**.

A FRIEZE OF VANISHING ANIMALS

This illustration brings together all 27 animals described in this book. It reminds us that they all had contact with humans at some point. It begins with giant animals from Australia and America (the giant echidna, *Megatherium*, and the *Glyptodon*), which lived among ancient humans. It ends with the Chinese river dolphin, which has only just been declared extinct, and Lonesome George, the last remaining member of a subspecies of Galapagos Island tortoise.